RECORD BREAKERS

MACHINES

AND INVENTIONS

DAVID JEFFERIS

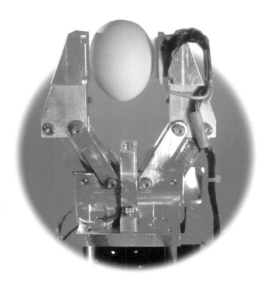

Belitha Press

First published in the UK in 2002 by

🦋 Belitha Press
A member of **Chrysalis** Books plc
64 Brewery Road, London N7 9NT

Design and editorial production
Alpha Communications
Copyright © David Jefferis 2002

ISBN 1 84138 425 9

British Library Cataloguing in Publication
Data for this book is available from the
British Library.

10 9 8 7 6 5 4 3 2 1

Acknowledgements
We wish to thank the following
individuals and organizations for their
help and assistance and for supplying
material in their collections:
Airbus Industrie, Alpha Archive,
Apple Corp, BMW Group, Boeing Corp,
Chrysler Corp, Deutsche Bahn AG,
Dyson Ltd, Ecotech, Electrolux Group,
Eurotunnel, Freedom Ship International
Inc, Fujitsu Corp, Honda Motor Co Ltd,
IBM Corp, Ron Jobson, Leicester City
Museums, Museum of British Road
Transport, NASA Space Agency, National
Ignition Facility Project, National Space
Centre, Nokia Corp, Panasonic Corp,
ResidenSea Ltd, Sony Corp,
SSC Programme Ltd, Toyota Corp,
Transrapid International, US Air Force,
US Marine Corps, US Navy,
Volkswagen AG, Ken Warby

Diagrams by Gavin Page
Project modelling by
Emily Stapleton-Jefferis
Educational advisor Julie Stapleton

We have checked the records in this
book but new ones are often added.

Printed in Taiwan

▲ The world's most expensive fighter jet is the US F-22 Raptor. There are plans for 295 of these jets to be built, at over $80 million each.

Previous page: A robot arm delicately holds an egg.

CONTENTS

✕ LOOK FOR THE TOOLS SYMBOL

Look for the hammer-and-spanner logo in boxes like this.
Here you will find extra facts and records.

WORLD OF MACHINES

▲ The first steam engine was built by Thomas Newcomen in 1712. Before long steam machines of all sorts were used everywhere, from factories to farms.

The way we live depends on machines, whether they are transport machines, labour-saving gadgets in our homes, computers, cameras or televisions.

The first machine was probably the wheel – we know that people in the Middle East about 5000 years ago used donkeys to pull carts. About the same time the ancient Egyptians farmed with ploughs, while the Greeks and Romans later developed screws, gears and pumps.

But the real machine age started only about 300 years ago. In the 1700s, inventors created hundreds of new machines, from steam trains to flush toilets.

◄ Automobile racing started not long after the car was invented, in 1885. This is the car that won the first official race in 1895. It went at a speed of 24 km/h.

Before the machine age, most people spent their lives working to survive. The idea of a holiday was almost unknown. Today labour-saving gadgets in our homes and at work give us time for hobbies, holidays and much else.

► This hand-worked wash tub and mangle was the latest home luxury 100 years ago.

Among the most recent inventions is the space rocket. Astronauts have already been to the Moon. There may be flights to distant planets in the future.

▲ The International Space Station is already the biggest machine in space. When fully assembled, it will be 108.5m long.

⚒ EARLY MACHINES TIMELINE

3000 BC In Asia carts with wheels are used. Ploughs are in use in Egypt.

100 BC Magnetic compass that points to the North Pole is invented in China.

1440s The printing press is perfected in Germany.

1500 A German locksmith, Peter Henlein, makes a clockwork pocket watch.

1590 Microscope built by Zacharias Janssen of Holland. The telescope is developed in 1608.

1712 First steam engine is built by Thomas Newcomen.

▼ Today's top-selling music system is the Sony Walkman, first produced in 1979. Over 200 million have been made so far.

SHIPS AND SUBS

▲ Clippers were the fastest cargo sail ships of the 1800s. The record was 596 km sailed in a day.

There are hundreds of different types of ship, but they fall into two main sorts – warships and commercial craft.

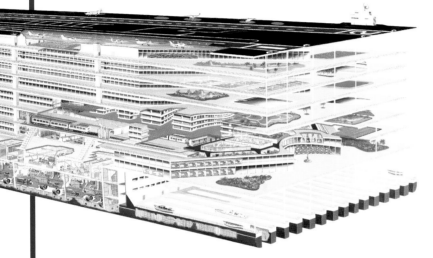

▲ The *Freedom Ship* could have parks, libraries, shops and even a small electric railway system.

The biggest ships today are oil-carrying supertankers, with the record being held by the *Jahre Viking*, which is 458m long and weighs over half a million tonnes.

But the *Jahre Viking* may be dwarfed by the *Freedom Ship*, if it is built. As planned, the craft will be 1317m long and will cruise the oceans with 115 000 passengers!

the Freedom Ship *compared to a normal ocean liner*

⚒ BIG AND SMALL

1911   The *France II* is launched. At 127m long, it is the biggest sailing ship ever built.

1991   The *Water Beatle* is launched, and is the world's smallest submarine. The tiny craft is just 2.95m long.

2001   *Adventure of the Seas* is the biggest cruise liner ever built, at 138 000 tonnes and carrying up to 3114 passengers.

The most powerful warships are aircraft carriers and submarines. The first nuclear-powered carrier was the 336m-long USS *Enterprise* of 1960. She was built to carry 5500 crew and over 90 aircraft at speeds of up to 65 km/h.

Below the waves, the Russian Typhoon is the biggest submarine ever built, with a length of about 170m and a 150-strong crew.

▲ A US nuclear-powered aircraft carrier leaves port with a full load of planes on display. Once at sea, aircraft are parked below. The deck is used for takeoffs and landings.

the Typhoon has two propellers and a single rudder

► A Typhoon sub weighs around 20 000 tonnes and carries a deadly load of missiles and torpedoes.

small fins, called hydroplanes, move the sub up or down when under water

TRAINS

Early railway record-breakers were powered by steam engines. Today the fastest trains use clean and quiet electric motors.

▲ The British *Mallard* is the fastest steam locomotive ever made. In 1938, the sleek machine pulled a seven-coach train at 203 km/h.

The first trains running along metal tracks were built in the early 1800s. They were used to move coal in mines in Wales. But soon, inventors were building trains that could take passengers. George Stephenson's *Rocket* of 1829 won a competition for reliability.

⚒ FASTER AND FASTER!

1804 The first steam engine runs on a track in Wales.

1829 Englishman George Stephenson wins a railway competition with his steam engine, the *Rocket*. It goes at nearly 47 km/h.

1893 The Empire State Express steam engine No '999' goes over 162 km/h near New York.

1903 A German Siemens electric train hits 210 km/h.

1964 The world's first regular train service to go at over 160 km/h is the Shinkansen express. It runs on Japan's Tokaido line.

1990 A French electric TGV train on a special run reaches 515 km/h.

2001 Work starts on a Transrapid line in China. When the line opens, trains will complete the 30 km route in only seven minutes.

▼ Powerful magnets allow the German Transrapid train to float just above a concrete track, enabling it to go faster than normal trains with wheels.

Transrapid uses a wide concrete track

Record-breaking trains today have electric motors, usually taking power from lines that run above the track. The TGV system in France has trains that run at 300 km/h. In future the German Transrapid may become as popular. In 2003, a Transrapid line in China will open, with speeds of 500 km/h or more.

▲ Spain's ICE-3 trains give the fastest regular service in Europe. They travel at 350 km/h from Madrid to Barcelona.

▼ Le Shuttle electric engines carry cars and trucks through the Eurotunnel that links Britain and France under the English Channel. The freight cars are the world's biggest, measuring up to 4.1m wide and 5.6m high.

metal arm takes power from overhead wires

▲ The US Model T Ford was the first car to be made on a production line. From 1908 to 1927, nearly 790 000 'tin lizzies' were made a year.

▼ Three record-breaking cars. From left to right, a Volkswagen Beetle, a Toyota Corolla and a Mini.

ON FOUR WHEELS

The first car was built in 1885 by the German engineer Karl Benz. Today millions of cars are made each year, in factories all over the world.

The most successful cars have been ordinary but reliable. The top-seller is the Toyota Corolla, from Japan, with over 23 million being produced since 1966. In that time, hundreds of improvements have been made, and the body style has been changed nine times. The runner-up is the German Volkswagen Beetle, which was designed before the Second World War – it's still being made in Mexico.

✗ TOP-SELLING CARS

1885 Karl Benz builds the first car with a petrol engine.

1908 The Model T Ford is the first car made on a production line. Over 16 million were made in all.

1937 Volkswagen Beetle is designed, and has been made ever since – over 21 million have been produced so far.

1959 The British Mini is the first really space-efficient car. Its sideways-mounted engine lets four adults sit in a tiny body.

1966 Toyota makes the Corolla. By 2001, it has become the best-selling car ever.

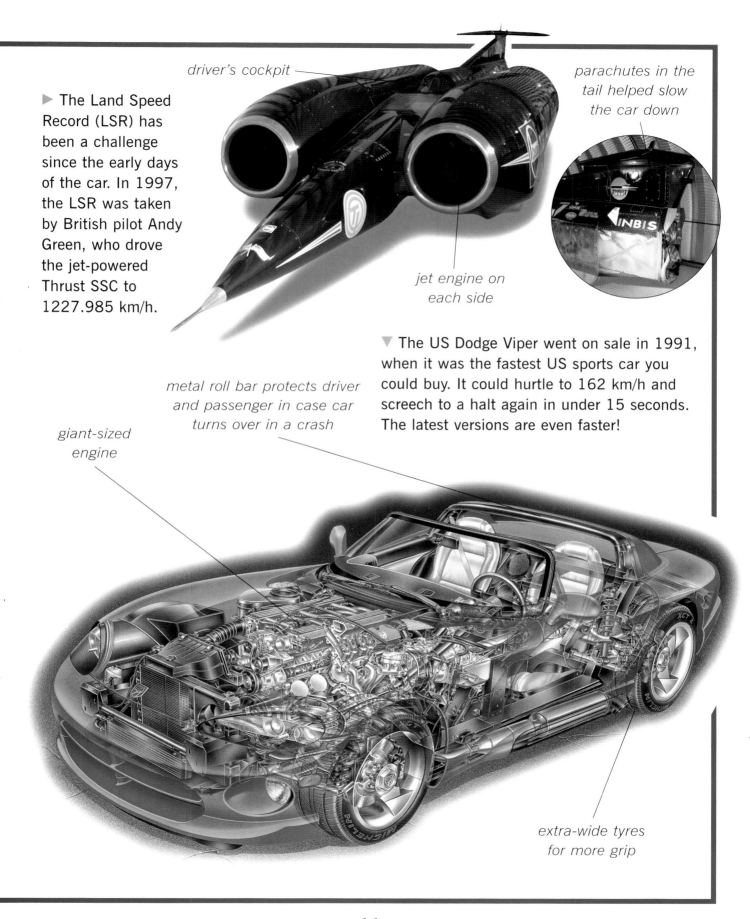

driver's cockpit

parachutes in the tail helped slow the car down

▶ The Land Speed Record (LSR) has been a challenge since the early days of the car. In 1997, the LSR was taken by British pilot Andy Green, who drove the jet-powered Thrust SSC to 1227.985 km/h.

jet engine on each side

▼ The US Dodge Viper went on sale in 1991, when it was the fastest US sports car you could buy. It could hurtle to 162 km/h and screech to a halt again in under 15 seconds. The latest versions are even faster!

metal roll bar protects driver and passenger in case car turns over in a crash

giant-sized engine

extra-wide tyres for more grip

FLYING MACHINES

▲ The pilot of the *Flyer* lay on the lower wing.

Aircraft have come a long way since the first flights of 1903. Today millions of people fly all over the world in jet airliners.

The first successful aircraft was the *Flyer* of 1903, built by Orville and Wilbur Wright. The Wright brothers made many flights, cruising at up to 48 km/h. In the 1920s and 1930s, other pilots and planes opened up world air routes. The world of passenger jet travel began with the British Comet of 1952. Today, the busiest long-distance route is between the cities of New York and London. About 3.3 million passengers fly on this route every year.

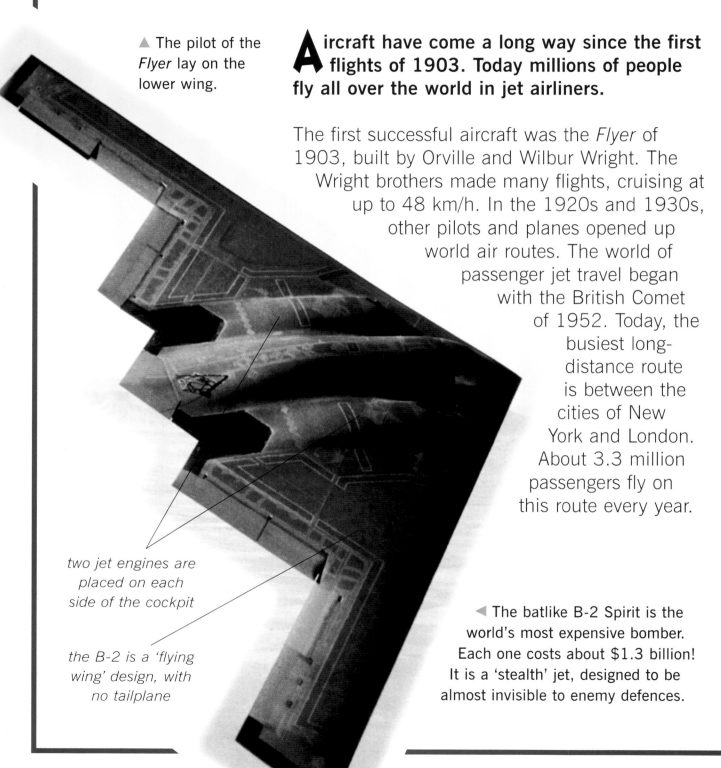

two jet engines are placed on each side of the cockpit

the B-2 is a 'flying wing' design, with no tailplane

◄ The batlike B-2 Spirit is the world's most expensive bomber. Each one costs about $1.3 billion! It is a 'stealth' jet, designed to be almost invisible to enemy defences.

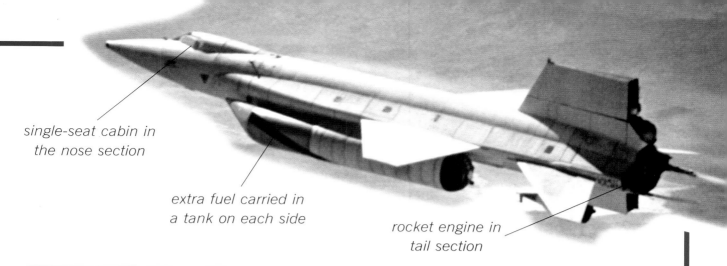

single-seat cabin in the nose section

extra fuel carried in a tank on each side

rocket engine in tail section

✘ FRONTIERS OF FLYING

1903 First flight, by Orville Wright, on 17 December. It lasts 12 seconds.

1909 Frenchman Louis Blériot flies across the English Channel, a distance of about 37 km.

1927 First non-stop flight from the USA to France, by Charles Lindbergh. The trip takes nearly 34 hours.

1939 First jet plane, the He 178, flies in Germany.

1976 Lockheed SR-71A becomes the fastest jet ever, at 3530 km/h.

1986 First non-stop flight around the world, by Dick Rutan and Jeana Yeager in *Voyager*.

▲ The X-15 rocket-plane still holds the record for the fastest, crewed aircraft flight. In 1967, William Knight flew the X-15 at 7277 km/h.

▶ The Airbus A380 will be the world's largest airliner when it goes into service in 2006. The huge jet will carry up to 555 pasengers. It sells for about $230 million.

JOURNEY INTO SPACE

◄ The crew of Apollo 11, the Moon-landing flight of 1969.

The first spacecraft was Sputnik 1, launched in 1957. Only 12 years later, humans landed on the Moon.

The Saturn V rocket was built for the Moon landing missions of the 1960s and 1970s. It is the biggest spacecraft ever built. At launch, the huge rocket weighed 2903 tonnes and stood 110.6m high.

The three astronauts sat in a tiny command module (CM) at the top – and this was the only part of the Apollo to return to Earth.

◄▼ The Saturn V command module (arrowed at left) had just enough room for three astronauts and their equipment.

command module was cone-shaped

command module landed in the sea after flight

▲ Today the Space Shuttle is the world's biggest crewed spacecraft. It is designed for a crew of up to seven. Here you can see a load in the big cargo bay.

Sputnik 1 had four radio antennas

⚒ LEAVING PLANET EARTH

1957 The first artificial satellite is launched. Russia's Sputnik 1 weighs 84 kg and is the size of a football.

1969 Astronauts Neil Armstrong and Edwin 'Buzz' Aldrin are the first humans on the Moon.

1971 Russia flies the first station in space. It is called Salyut 1 and weighs over 18 tonnes.

1961 Russian cosmonaut Yuri Gagarin is the first human in space.

1981 US Space Shuttle's first flight.

1999 First section of the International Space Station (ISS) is placed in space by the crew of a Space Shuttle.

COMMUNICATION MACHINES

Communicating long distances was once a matter of sending a letter, then waiting weeks for a reply. Today's electronic machines make this almost instant.

▲ The Wheatstone telegraph was used in 1839 for a 22-km line in Britain.

◀ The first radio show was broadcast by the US station KDKA in 1921. By 1930, there were thousands of stations across the world.

The ancestor of the today's Internet was the telegraph of the nineteenth century. The telegraph was as exciting then as the Internet is today. You could send a long-distance message along a telegraph wire in minutes instead of days or weeks.

Television started in 1932, with broadcasts by the BBC in Britain.

▶ This is an early portable television from the 1950s. It was still a big machine, as the equipment used was still very heavy and bulky.

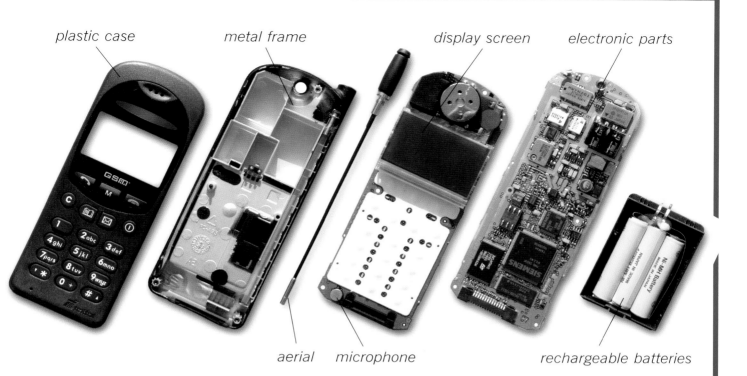

plastic case   metal frame   display screen   electronic parts

aerial   microphone   rechargeable batteries

Mobile phones and the Internet have transformed the way many of us live. Most people now have a computer in the home, so they can get on to the Internet easily. And mobile phones are even more popular – in Finland, 70 per cent of adults have one or more mobile phones.

▲ Mobile phones are jam-packed with electronics. Many mobiles can also link to the Internet.

✖ INTERNET RECORDS

1969 Early form of Internet, the ARPAnet is launched as a military communications system.

1972 US computer programmer Ray Tomlinson devises first e-mail program.

1989 The World Wide Web is demonstrated.

1994 There are now over 10 000 websites and a pizza can be bought online.

1996 More than 500 000 websites are online.

2000 Internet advertising rises by almost half over 1999 – advertisers spend a record $2.9 billion.

2001 Several electronic companies develop watches that can also play music from the Internet.

watch/music player weighs only 43g

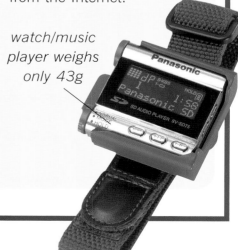

HOME INVENTIONS

▲ The first sewing machine was patented in 1851 by Isaac Merritt Singer. It was driven by pushing a foot pedal. By 1976, you could get an electronic sewing machine that could sew in 25 different stitch patterns.

In the past, homes had very few machines. Today, most houses are packed from top to bottom with high-tech gadgets.

Until the twentieth century, lots of time was spent doing the chores – a day for washing, a day for cleaning and so on. What changed things was mains electricity (first available in 1882), which was a good source of power for many labour-saving gadgets in the home.

One early electric invention was the toaster. In 1905, an engineer called Albert Marsh made wire using a mixture of metals that glowed hot but did not break easily. Just a few years after this discovery dozens of models of toaster were on sale.

◄ Electric washing machines were first made in the 1920s, though clothes were dried by rolling them in a hand wringer.

► The first spin dryer of 1957 weighed 300 kg. By 2001, the most powerful model weighed just 91 kg.

drum has 4923 holes to get rid of water quickly

Internet screen is built into door of fridge

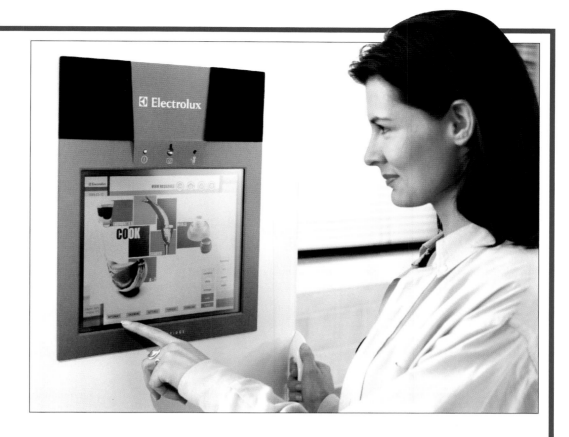

Refrigerators were first sold in 1913, and big sales brought prices down – in 1920 a fridge cost around $600. Nine years later the price was less than half this. In 2001, an Internet-linked refrigerator cost around £5000. Soon such a link could be included as standard.

▲ This refrigerator was the first to have an Internet link. Food can be ordered when supplies run low.

🔧 MAKING HOMES EASIER TO LOOK AFTER

1882 US inventor Thomas Edison starts the first electric power station in New York. It supplies 225 homes.

1913 First refrigerator made for use in the home.

1929 First kitchen sink waste-disposal unit is developed by the US company General Electric.

1932 First electric dishwasher goes on sale.

1947 First microwave cooker goes on sale, named the 'Radarange'. Early ones are as big as a refrigerator.

1955 First home deep-freeze goes on sale, with smaller versions being made a few years later.

1980s Computer controls start to be included in most household appliances, making them cheaper and more reliable.

COMPUTERS

Early computers were very big, but were no better than a modern pocket calculator. Today's computers are smaller, cheaper and more powerful.

▲ The first computer was Colossus, built in 1943. It was made to break secret message codes in the Second World War.

In 1943, the boss of the IBM company predicted that the world might need 'maybe five computers'. He might have been right if computers had stayed large, but their shrinking size and price has put them in every area of our lives. Experts think that there are now about 600 million computers worldwide!

► Most new computers break performance records. Apart from its regular computer functions, this 2001 laptop model plays music and video discs, and can edit home movies.

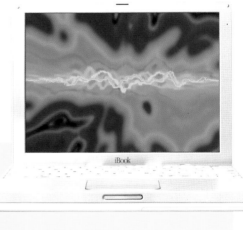

ADVANCE OF THE COMPUTER

1943 Colossus code-cracking computer used in the Second World War. Also in 1943, works starts on the US ENIAC. It uses a set of instructions, the ancestor of programs today.

1954 General Electric is the first company to use a computer, a Univac model.

1981 The first personal computer is made by the US IBM company.

1984 Apple Macintosh computer uses a point-and-click screen display, with a mouse. This helps make computers easier to use.

1993 Computers are used to make realistic-looking dinosaurs in the Hollywood movie *Jurassic Park*.

2000 The computer game *Super Mario Brothers* is the best-selling game, with more than 40 million copies sold.

▲ Computers are in charge on the Space Shuttle. Landings are computer-controlled, all the way from space to the runway.

In aircraft and spacecraft, computers are used to show flight information in the cockpit. Video screens are used to show speed, height, position and other information. The equipment is far more reliable than the old-fashioned mechanical equipment that used dials and pointers.

▼ In 1997, the IBM *Deep Blue* computer was the first machine to beat a human in a series of chess games.

the first chess programs were made for home computers in the 1980s

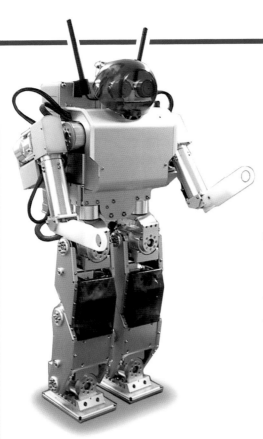

▲ The latest walking robot is the 48-cm tall Fujitsu HOAP. It can be controlled by signals from a laptop computer.

ROBOTS

Robots used to be the stuff of sci-fi stories. Now they are made for real-life jobs.

▲ C3PO is one of the most famous sci-fi movie robots.

For many years the word 'robot' has been used for almost any machine that works by itself, without needing constant attention. For example, in car factories robot machines do precise jobs such as welding or painting.

In 1996, the Japanese Honda company built the P2 robot. It was the first human-like robot that could walk properly without falling over.

Aibo-type robot dog barks, walks and wags its tail

 REIGN OF THE ROBOTS

1893 US engineer George Moore makes a steam-powered 'walking man' that can walk at 14.5 km/h.

1948 US researcher Grey Walter builds electronic robot 'tortoises' that can go by themselves to a mains plug for a battery recharge.

1968 A small, wheeled robot called Shakey learns to find its way out of a maze.

1972 Unimation becomes the first company to make industrial robot equipment.

1996 The Honda P2 robot can walk up and down

stairs, and can keep its balance if pushed sideways. The P3 model of 1997 can also walk over obstacles.

2000 The Sony Aibo robot dog goes on sale. It is very popular – in a few minutes some 3000 Aibos have been sold, at $2000 each.

▶ Here metal parts of a car are welded together by an industrial robot. These machines do not have complete bodies. For this job, only an arm is needed.

▲ The Honda P2 had batteries that lasted just 20 minutes.

▲ In 1997, the first remote-controlled roving vehicle landed on the planet Mars. Future rovers, such as the one shown here, will be robots that can steer themselves around rocks and craters.

viewing area

POWER MACHINES

The race is on to find and use new sources of power before oil, gas and coal run out. And the cleaner these energy sources are, the better.

Many scientists agree that wind power is a good way to provide energy, as it produces no pollution. The giant wind turbine shown here is an Enercon E-66, claimed by its German makers to be the most efficient machine of its kind in the world.

The E-66 is huge, with three 30.8m-long blades, yet it takes only a few days to assemble. This one produces enough electricity for about 3000 people living in the town of Swaffham in Britain.

◀ Visitors climb 305 steps to a viewing area.

▶ On a fine day the view is fantastic.

⚒ MACHINES THAT MAKE CLEAN ENERGY

1981 World's largest wind farm is built in California, USA, with 6000 turbines.

1993 British inventor Trevor Baylis devises a radio that uses clockwork for power instead of batteries.

1998 Wind power is the fastest growing source of energy in the world.

2000 The biggest users of solar energy are Switzerland, Germany and Japan.

2001 Most Israelis use solar-powered water heaters.

▲ Researchers check the huge research laser for a test. The beams will fire through the holes.

Scientists are trying another way to make clean energy, with this laser machine. It is the biggest of its kind in the world. A laser is a beam of light that can be made strong enough to burn through steel. The machine's 192 lasers will fire at a pellet of fuel to make energy hotter than the Sun!

▲ 20 000 of these clockwork-powered radios are made every month. One winding charges a battery for about 40 minutes of radio.

▲ The box camera was the first popular type.

MACHINE RECORDS

Here are some facts and records from the world of machines and inventions.

SAY CHEESE!

The very first photograph was taken in 1827 by Joseph Niépce from France. It was a very fuzzy view from a window in his home. In 1888, the American George Eastman produced the easy-to-use Kodak camera. To get prints you posted the camera to Kodak. The firm removed the film, then processed it and sent the prints back.

CLEVER INVENTOR

The American Thomas Edison (1847-1931) is reckoned as the world's greatest inventor. He thought up or improved over 1000 machines. These included the phonograph, microphone and light bulb.

MUSCLES IN FLIGHT

The first powered flight was by Orville Wright in 1903. But it took until 1979 before a human-powered aircraft was successful. The first long flight was by US cyclist Bryan Allen, who pedalled *Gossamer Albatross* across the English Channel. The plane had a wingspan of nearly 29m, but weighed just 25 kg!

BIG TELESCOPES

The biggest telescope in space is the Hubble Space Telescope (HST). It is as big as a school bus and has been taking pictures of stars and planets since 1990. On Earth, the Keck telescope in Hawaii is the biggest. Its light-collecting mirror is made of 36 hexagons that link up like a honeycomb.

◄ The first combat jet able to take off and land vertically is the Harrier. It was developed from the British experimental P1127, which first flew in October 1960.

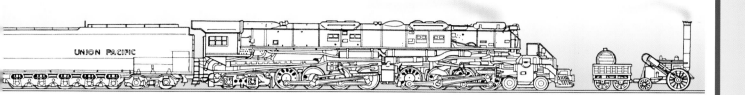

▲ The US 'Big Boy' locomotives were the biggest steam locomotives ever made, weighing over 500 tonnes. Big Boys could haul 5000 tonnes of freight. The pioneer *Rocket* of 1829 is shown right.

KEEP WALKING!

Trevor Baylis, who invented the clockwork-powered radio and torch, has also devised shoes that generate electricity. In 2000, walking tests proved that they could give enough power for a mobile phone.

CAR CRAZY WORLD?

In the year 1900, there were about 50 000 motor vehicles worldwide. By 2000, there were over 650 million! But new vehicles are cleaner than older models, so there is less pollution than in the 1960s.

GREAT GAME MACHINE

The best-selling computer game machine of 2000 was the Sony Playstation 2 (PS2). In the first two days on sale, 980 000 PS2s were sold. But the Game Boy is also very successful – Nintendo has made 115 million so far.

FASTEST COMPUTER

In 2001, Compaq produced the Terascale computer, which became the world's fastest, able to perform 6 trillion (or 6 000 000 000 000) calculations per second.

ROBOT WORLD

Japan leads the world in using industrial robots. Worldwide, there are about 750 000 robots in factories – and Japan has more than half of them. Also, Japanese robot researchers see a big future for robots, such as using them to help patients in hospitals and assisting old people.

◄ Fastest human on water is the Australian Ken Warby. In 1978, he raced to more than 511 km/h. He now has a new boat (left) which could be even faster.

▲ The highest jet flight was by a Russian MiG-25 which achieved 37 650m in 1977. Now you can buy a passenger flight aboard a MiG-25 – but it costs about $12 000!

▲ This robot animal was featured online in 2001.

MACHINE WORDS

Here are some words used in this book that you may not know.

CLIPPER

A type of sailing ship built for speed, before the days of steamships. Clippers raced in the 1800s, especially to carry tea from China to Europe.

E-MAIL

Short for electronic mail. The system that sends messages between computers, using the the Internet as the carrier.

INTERNET

A system that links computers worldwide. Signals may pass along telephone wires, cables or by radio. The Internet also includes the World Wide Web, which shows information on websites – these fill a screen with words, pictures and often sounds and movies.

► Laser beams can be seen here as coloured straight lines.

LASER

A type of light beam that stays focused very tightly, rather than fanning out like the light from a torch.

NUCLEAR POWER

Type of energy that uses the very hot (and dangerous) metal uranium to boil water. The resulting steam can be used to make electricity. Aircraft carriers and military submarines are two ships that use this form of power.

PHONOGRAPH

The earliest machine that could record sound, invented by Thomas Edison in 1877.

PRODUCTION LINE

A way of making cars (and other machines) using a slowly moving line, on which parts are added as the line progresses. A car usually starts with an empty metal body shell, to which seats, engine, wheels and other parts are added. Many car factories produce hundreds of vehicles a day on their production lines.

PROGRAM

A set of instructions that tells a computer to do a particular job. There are thousands of programs. Examples are ones for word processing, graphics or computer games.

ROBOT

A machine that can do certain tasks without needing much attention. The word comes from the Czech 'robota' which means 'work'. Science-fiction robots usually look something like metal people. One famous example is C3PO, the robot from the movie *Star Wars*.

SATELLITE

Any space object that circles around, or orbits, another. It may be a natural satellite, such as the Earth's Moon, or a human-made, artificial one. Examples of these include the International Space Station (ISS) and Russian Sputniks.

SOLAR POWER

A machine that can extract the energy from sunlight. Some solar systems use the Sun's heat to warm water. Others are made of special materials that convert energy in the light to electricity.

STEALTH

A military aircraft that is built to be nearly invisible to enemy detection systems.

TELEGRAPH

A communications system that came before the telephone. It also used wires, but could send and receive only coded signals, not speech.

▲ Some mobile phones now use Internet links to show pictures as well as sound.

TGV

A special railway system that has been built across France. The letters 'TGV' stand for 'Train à Grande Vitesse' or high-speed train.

WELDING

A method of joining metals together by melting them at the joining edges.

WIND TURBINE

Any modern machine that extracts energy from the wind. There are many different designs, but most of them use sails that look like aircraft propellers. A group of wind turbines built close together is called a wind farm.

◄ This type of TGV train is called a Duplex. It has decks on two levels, a café and even a changing room for babies.

MACHINE PROJECTS

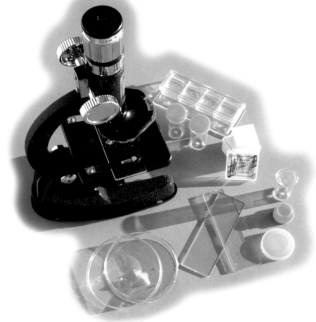

These experiments show you some simple machine science.

Microscopes have been around for more than 400 years. Today's optical equipment also includes telescopes and binoculars.

They are all based on the same idea – glass lenses are used to bend light and give a magnified, or enlarged, image.

▲ A simple microscope gives young scientists a good start in their studies. The other tools are used to prepare specimens.

▶ These binoculars are small enough to carry in your pocket.

MAKE A WATER-DROP MICROSCOPE

This little machine uses the naturally curved shape of a water drop to bend light like the lens of a microscope. You will use it to magnify a printed picture and so see the pattern of small printed dots which makes up the image.

1 You need a card rectangle, a hole-puncher, modelling clay, a can and a printed picture.

2 Line up the card in the hole puncher. Press out a hole in one end of the card.

REDUCING FRICTION

Oil is used in many machines to allow parts to slide easily against each other. A thin film of oil keeps them slightly apart, reducing the rubbing action called friction.

◀ Oil is used to keep car engines and many other moving parts working smoothly.

1 You need a screw-top jar and washing-up liquid. Unscrew the top, then tighten it. Feel how your hand grips the lid.

2 Squeeze some oily washing-up liquid over the lid. Now try and open it. Your hand should slip now that the friction is much less.

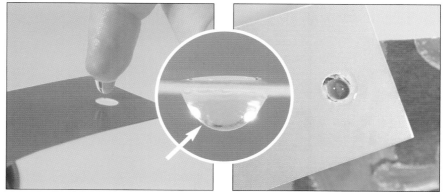

3 Lay the card on top of the can. Fix it firmly into place with the modelling clay.

4 Carefully place a drop of water in the hole. It should form the lens shape arrowed.

5 Hold the printed picture underneath the water drop and spot the dots.

INDEX